This Book Belongs to:

_____

3 Stories in one

BIBLE HEROES
STORYBOOK

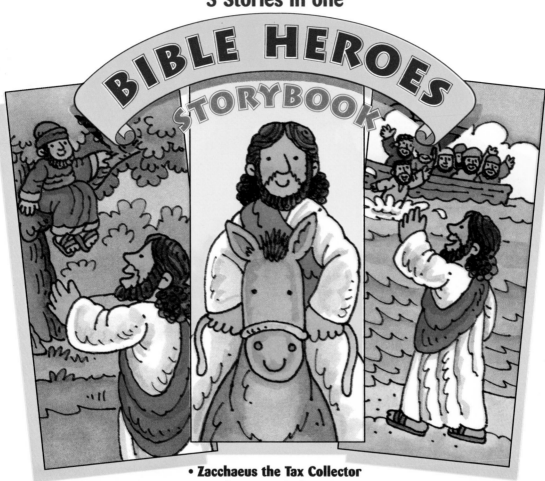

- **Zacchaeus the Tax Collector**
  - **The Triumphal Entry**
  - **The Resurrection of Jesus**

ZACCHAEUS the TAX COLLECTOR

Retold by Andy Rector

Illustrated by Ben Mahan

In the days of Jesus, the Roman Empire ruled much of the known world. An Emperor lived in Rome and collected money from all the other countries Rome conquered. Judea—the land where Jesus lived—was one of these countries.

The Emperor hired tax collectors to take money from the countries that he ruled. Zacchaeus collected taxes. He lived in a town called Jericho and collected taxes for the Emperor from his own people. No one liked him because he cheated them.

"That Zacchaeus," they would say. "He collects too much money. He keeps much of it for himself and what he doesn't keep he gives to the Emperor. He is a traitor to his own people!"

One day Jesus walked through Jericho. Crowds gathered around Jesus and followed him down the street. They had heard of the many miracles he had performed.

Zacchaeus looked out the window to see who was making all the noise. "What's going on?" he asked a man passing by. "What is this crowd doing?"

"Trying to see Jesus," said the man who was swept away by the crowd.

"I've heard of Jesus," said Zacchaeus. "I'd like to see him for myself."

When Zacchaeus walked outside he tried to see over the heads of the people crowding around Jesus. Zacchaeus, however, stood much shorter than the other people. "I can't see Jesus!" said Zacchaeus.

"Get lost," said some people who did not like him.

"How am I going to see Jesus?" Zacchaeus thought. Then he had an idea.

Zacchaeus saw which way the crowds were moving. "Jesus must be heading in that direction," he said.

Then Zacchaeus ran ahead of the crowd and climbed up a sycamore fig tree. He sat out on one of the limbs and waited for Jesus to walk by the tree.

Soon Jesus walked by the sycamore fig tree. The people surrounded Jesus and wanted to ask him questions about God. Suddenly Jesus stopped right below the tree. He looked up.

"Zacchaeus, come down from that tree," said Jesus.

"Are you talking to me?" asked Zacchaeus.

"Yes Zacchaeus, come down. I must stay at your house today."

No one ever wanted to visit Zacchaeus! Why would Jesus want to stay with a man who cheated people?

But Zacchaeus said to Jesus, "I will give half of my money to the poor and if I have cheated anyone out of money, I will pay them four times what I took."

"God wants you to be a good person, Zacchaeus," said Jesus. "I came to find those who are doing wrong."

Jesus visited Zacchaeus that day and they talked long into the night. From that day forth, Zacchaeus stopped cheating people out of money and told everyone he met about the wonderful man named Jesus.

THE
TRIUMPHAL ENTRY

Retold by Andy Rector

Illustrated by Ben Mahan

One day Jesus and his close friends walked towards a town that was called Jerusalem. They went there every year at that time to celebrate with a feast. Suddenly outside the city gates of Jerusalem, Jesus stopped. He had decided to send some of his followers ahead. He had a job for them.

He said, "Go to the town. You will see a donkey tied there, which no on has ridden. Untie it and bring it back to me. If anyone asks you why you are taking the donkey, just tell them, 'The Lord needs it.'"

The followers looked surprised, but they did as he asked. They ran ahead to find the donkey.

The followers went into the city.

"Look," said one of them. "There's a donkey tied to the house over there, just like Jesus said."

"How did he know there would be a donkey?" asked another.

"Because he is Jesus," said a third follower.

They untied the donkey. Suddenly two young men walked around the corner.

"What are you doing with our donkey?" one of the young men asked.

"The Lord needs it," the followers said.

"Fine," said the young man. "You may borrow it."

The friends of Jesus returned with the donkey.

"It was just like you said, Jesus," the followers exclaimed.

Jesus got on the donkey and rode into the town of Jerusalem. Many people had come to visit Jerusalem that day for the feast. When the people saw Jesus riding down the middle of the streets of Jerusalem on a donkey, they gathered palm branches and began to wave them in the air.

Suddenly the crowd began to chant, "Hosanna! Hosanna!" Others shouted, "Blessed is he who comes in the name of the Lord!"

As Jesus rode the donkey through town, the crowds cheered and chanted for a long time. The followers of Jesus became a little nervous.

"What's going on?" one follower asked another. "Why are the people making a fuss over Jesus?"

But none of them knew what to make of the scene.

"The crowd is chanting things from the scriptures," said one of the followers.

"Yes!" said another follower. "They are talking about Jesus!"

One group of men stood behind the crowd and grumbled. They called themselves the Pharisees.

"I've had enough of this Jesus," said a Pharisee. "The people should be paying attention to us, not him."

"I know," said another. "We're the teachers of the scriptures. We should be getting the praise."

So the Pharisees began to think of a way they could get rid of Jesus.

THE RESURRECTION
of JESUS

Retold by Andy Rector

Illustrated by Ben Mahan

The Pharisees gathered in the dark corners of the temple one evening. They had found a way to get rid of Jesus.

"Where is he?" asked one of the Pharisees.

"He said he would be here," said another Pharisee. "Don't worry. He'll be here."

Soon, a follower of Jesus named Judas walked up to the Pharisees. "I know where Jesus is. If I lead you to him will you pay me?"

"Yes," said the Pharisees. "We will pay you thirty pieces of silver."

"Follow me," said Judas.

The Pharisees and some Roman soldiers followed after Judas.

Later that night Jesus and three of his followers, Peter, James and John, went to the Garden of Gethsemane. "Sit here and pray," said Jesus. "I am going somewhere else to pray."

Jesus knew that Judas would betray him into the hands of the Pharisees. When he came back he found the followers asleep. "Wake up and pray!" said Jesus. He went off to pray again and when he returned he found them asleep again. He woke them up.

Suddenly Judas walked up from the shadows and kissed Jesus. This was a signal to the Pharisees and Jesus was soon surrounded.

The followers became frightened and ran away, leaving Jesus alone in the hands of the Pharisees and the wicked soldiers.

The Pharisees sent Jesus to stand trial before the Roman governor, Pilate. "I don't understand," said Pilate. "What has this man done wrong?"

"He claims to be our king!" cried the Pharisees. "He claims to be God!"

"I don't see him as a bad person," said Pilate, but the crowd screamed for the death of Jesus. "Fine, I will do as you ask," said Pilate.

Soon Jesus was tortured and beaten. "So, you claim to be our king?" said the Roman soldiers. They made a crown out of sharp thorns and put it on Jesus's head. "Now the king has his crown!" they laughed. "Hail, hail the king!"

After mocking him, they made Jesus carry a heavy piece of wood which was shaped like a cross. He carried it up a hill called Calvary. On that hill they stood the wooden cross

up like a pole and nailed the hands and feet of Jesus onto the wood.

Jesus hung from the cross in pain. He said to God, "Father, forgive them for they don't know what they do." Then Jesus died. Some friends of Jesus took his body off the cross and buried him in a cave.

The friends and followers of Jesus missed him. They heard rumors that Jesus lived, but they were not sure what to believe.

One night the close followers of Jesus ate a meal behind locked doors. Suddenly Jesus appeared to them out of nowhere.

"Peace be with you!" said Jesus. The followers could not believe it. Jesus lived. Soon Jesus disappeared again.

Some time later the followers were out fishing one morning. Suddenly Jesus joined them on the beach. They had seen Jesus die with their own eyes, and yet here he was with them again.

"Lord," they said to Jesus, "we are sorry for running away from you when you were arrested. We know now that you are God's son."

"You are forgiven," said Jesus. And so the followers had breakfast with Jesus that morning on the beach.